How to Start a Side Hustle in 30 Days or Less

Learn How to Make Money Online, Become Your Own Boss, and Achieve Financial Freedom Through Freelancing, Dropshipping, and E-Commerce

The Fix-It Guy

Table of Contents

This isn't your typical business manual, it's your backstage pass to the world of freelancing, dropshipping, and e-commerce, strategies that have transformed ordinary people into extraordinary success stories.

Introduction

Hey there, aspiring entrepreneur! Ever dreamt of breaking free from the 9-to-5 grind, making money online, and having the freedom to live life on your terms? Well, buckle up because you're about to embark on an exhilarating journey toward financial independence, and I'm here to be your guide.

Imagine a life where you call the shots, where your bank account isn't just a number but a testament to your hard work and creativity. Picture waking up each morning with excitement, knowing that your hustle isn't just a side gig, it's the key to unlocking the door to your dreams. Whether you want to travel the world, spend more time with your loved ones, or simply relish the thrill of building something from scratch, this book is your ticket to that destination.

In "How to Start a Side Hustle in 30 Days or Less," we're not just talking about vague concepts and wishful thinking. No, we're diving headfirst into the nitty-gritty details, the actionable steps, and the insider secrets that will turn your passion into profit. This isn't your typical business manual; it's your backstage pass to the world of freelancing, dropshipping, and e-commerce, strategies that have transformed ordinary people into extraordinary success stories.

Why should you listen to me? Well, because I've been where you are right now, craving change, hungry for success, and wondering if there's a way out of the mundane. I've faced the challenges, celebrated the victories, and learned the ropes through trial and error. And now, I'm here to share everything I know so that you can fast-track your journey and avoid the pitfalls that often trip up newcomers.

Get ready to roll up your sleeves and get your hands dirty because building a side hustle isn't just about making money; it's about creating a lifestyle that resonates with who you truly are. It's about turning your passion into profit, one sale at a time. So, are you ready to embrace the freedom, the excitement, and the endless possibilities that come with being your own boss?

If your answer is a resounding "YES," then let's dive in and make your side hustle dreams a reality. Your adventure begins now, let's make it epic!

Chapter 1

Getting Started

Defining Your Niche

In the exhilarating world of entrepreneurship, the first step is often the most crucial one, defining your niche. Your niche isn't just a category; it's your unique corner of the market, your specialized area of expertise that sets you apart from the competition. It's not merely what you sell; it's how you sell it, whom you sell it to, and why they should buy it from you.

Why Is Defining Your Niche Important?

Imagine walking into a vast, bustling marketplace filled with stalls selling everything from handmade crafts to cutting-edge gadgets. Now, picture yourself trying to sell something without a clear idea of what makes your product or service special. That's where defining your niche comes in. It helps you narrow down your focus, enabling you to target the right audience effectively. Here's why it's crucial:

1. Targeted Marketing: Knowing your niche allows you to tailor your marketing efforts specifically to the people who are most likely to buy from you. This targeted approach increases your chances of attracting the right customers.

2. Establishing Expertise: Specializing in a particular niche allows you to become an expert in that field. Customers are more likely to trust and buy from someone who demonstrates in-depth knowledge and passion for what they're offering.

3. Reducing Competition: By finding a unique angle or a specific market segment, you can reduce direct competition. Instead of competing with a broad range of businesses, you're competing within a smaller, more defined space.

4. Building a Brand: Your niche becomes an integral part of your brand identity. It's what people remember you for, making it easier for them to recall your business when they need products or services related to your niche.

How to Define Your Niche:

1. Identify Your Passions and Skills: Start by listing your passions, hobbies, and skills. What are you genuinely enthusiastic about? What are you good at?

Your niche should align with your interests and expertise to keep you motivated and engaged in your business.

2. Research the Market: Analyze the market to identify gaps or underserved areas. Look for opportunities where your skills and passion intersect with market demand. Conduct surveys, read industry reports, and study your competitors to gain insights.

3. Evaluate Profitability: While passion is essential, your niche should also be profitable. Research the pricing and demand for products or services within your potential niche. Ensure there's a sustainable market that can support your business financially.

4. Define Your Unique Selling Proposition (USP): Your USP is what sets you apart from the competition. It could be the quality of your products, exceptional customer service, innovative solutions, or a combination of factors. Clearly define what makes your business special and why customers should choose you.

5. Test and Refine: Once you've identified your niche, test your ideas on a small scale. Launch a pilot project or a limited product line to gauge customer response. Use feedback to refine your offerings and marketing strategies.

Remember, defining your niche is not a one-time task; it's an ongoing process. Stay attuned to market trends, customer feedback, and your passions, and be willing to adapt and evolve your niche as your business grows.

By honing in on your niche, you're not just finding a market; you're carving out your space in the entrepreneurial landscape. Embrace your uniqueness, and let it guide you toward building a successful and fulfilling side hustle. Your journey starts with defining your niche, so go ahead, find your passion, and make it your business.

Market Research and Analysis

Before you dive headlong into your side hustle journey, it's imperative to understand the heartbeat of your potential customers. Market research and analysis are your compass, guiding you toward the right direction by uncovering what people want, need, and are willing to pay for.

Why Market Research Matters:
Imagine launching a product or service without knowing whether there's a demand for it. It's like setting sail without a map in uncharted waters. Market research mitigates this risk by providing valuable insights into your target audience:

1. Understanding Customer Needs: Market research allows you to identify gaps in the market. By understanding what your potential customers are looking for, you can tailor your offerings to meet their needs effectively.

2. Analyzing Competition: Researching competitors helps you discern what works and what doesn't in your niche. It enables you to differentiate your business, offering unique value propositions that set you apart from others.

3. Pricing Strategies: Through market analysis, you can determine the right price point for your products or services. Understanding what customers are willing to pay helps you strike a balance between profitability and customer satisfaction.

4. Identifying Trends: Markets are dynamic, with trends constantly evolving. Research helps you stay ahead of the curve, allowing you to adapt your offerings to align with current and future market trends.

Market Research Methods:

1. Surveys and Questionnaires: Create targeted surveys to gather feedback from potential customers. Ask questions about their preferences, pain points, and willingness to pay. Analyze the responses to identify patterns and trends.

2. Interviews: Conduct one-on-one interviews with individuals within your target audience. Personal conversations can reveal nuanced insights that might be missed in surveys.

3. Social Media Listening: Monitor social media platforms for discussions related to your niche. Social media listening tools can help you gauge sentiment, identify trends, and understand customer opinions.

4. Competitor Analysis: Study your competitors, both big players and similar-sized businesses. Analyze their products, pricing, marketing strategies, and customer reviews to identify strengths and weaknesses.

Choosing Your Side Hustle Model

With market research in hand, it's time to select the side hustle model that aligns best with your skills, interests, and market demand. There's no one-size-fits-all approach; your choice will depend on various factors, including your expertise, available resources, and the level of involvement you desire.

Freelancing: Ideal for individuals with specific skills (such as writing, graphic design, programming) who prefer offering services on a project basis. Freelancers often work independently, taking on clients and projects based on their expertise.

Dropshipping: A popular e-commerce model where you sell products without holding inventory. When a customer makes a purchase, the product is shipped directly from the supplier to the customer. Dropshipping reduces upfront costs and inventory management hassles.

E-Commerce: Involves selling physical or digital products directly to customers through an online store. E-commerce entrepreneurs handle product sourcing, inventory management, and shipping. It offers more control but requires careful planning and investment in inventory.

Affiliate Marketing: Affiliate marketers promote other people's products and earn a commission for every sale made through their referral. This model requires strong marketing skills and the ability to drive traffic to affiliate partners' products.

Subscription Services: Entrepreneurs create subscription-based services, providing customers with recurring value. This model often involves delivering products, content, or services regularly in exchange for a subscription fee.

Conclusion: Your Path to Side Hustle Success

Market research and choosing the right side hustle model are the cornerstones of your entrepreneurial journey. Armed with insights from your research, and a clear understanding of your chosen path, you're equipped to make informed decisions, cater to your audience's needs, and build a profitable venture.

Remember, entrepreneurship is an ongoing learning experience. Stay open to feedback, adapt to market changes, and continuously refine your approach. Your side hustle adventure is unique to you, embrace the challenge, learn from your experiences, and let your passion drive you toward success. The world of possibilities awaits, it's time to turn your dreams into your reality.

Chapter 2

Freelancing Your Way to Success

Building Your Freelance Skillset

Freelancing offers the freedom to work on your terms, setting your own hours, choosing your clients, and honing your skills in a field you're passionate about. But to succeed in the competitive freelancing landscape, you need more than just a desire to work independently, you need a set of marketable skills that clients are eager to pay for.

Identifying Your Freelance Skills:

1. Assess Your Strengths: Reflect on your talents, expertise, and experiences. What are you exceptionally good at? Your skills can range from writing and graphic design to programming and digital marketing. Identify the skills you enjoy using, as enthusiasm often translates into high-quality work.

2. Research Market Demand: Investigate the demand for specific freelance skills within your niche. Websites like job boards, freelance platforms, and industry forums can provide insights into the skills that clients are actively seeking.

3. Continuous Learning: The digital landscape evolves rapidly. Stay updated with the latest tools, technologies, and trends related to your field. Invest in online courses, workshops, and certifications to enhance your skills and stay competitive.

4. Networking: Engage with professionals in your industry. Attend conferences, webinars, and networking events. Interacting with peers can provide valuable insights, mentorship, and potential collaboration opportunities.

Creating an Online Portfolio

Your online portfolio is your digital storefront – a showcase of your skills, expertise, and the quality of your work. It's the first impression you make on potential clients, so it's crucial to present your best work in a compelling and professional manner.

Portfolio Essentials:

1. Select Your Best Work: Curate a selection of your most impressive and diverse projects. Focus on quality over quantity. Highlight projects that demonstrate your expertise and versatility.

2. Craft Engaging Descriptions: For each project, provide detailed descriptions outlining your role, the challenges faced, and the solutions implemented. Explain the impact of your work on the client's goals or business.

3. Visual Appeal: Use high-quality images, videos, or interactive elements to showcase your work. Invest in professional photography or design to make your portfolio visually appealing and easy to navigate.

4. Client Testimonials: If available, include testimonials from satisfied clients. Positive feedback adds credibility and reassures potential clients of your reliability and professionalism.

5. Contact Information: Clearly display your contact information, including email address, phone number, and links to your professional social media profiles. Make it easy for clients to get in touch with you.

Showcasing Your Expertise: Beyond the Portfolio
While your portfolio is a powerful tool, your expertise should extend beyond static examples of your work. Consider creating valuable content such as blog posts, tutorials, or case studies related to your field. Sharing your knowledge not only positions you as an authority but also attracts potential clients who value your expertise.

Remember, building a successful freelance career takes time, dedication, and a commitment to continuous improvement. Invest in your skills, create a compelling portfolio, and showcase your expertise to the world. With the right mindset and a passion for your craft, you'll be well on your way to freelancing your way to success.

Finding Freelance Gigs

Finding freelance gigs in the vast digital landscape might seem daunting, but with the right approach and a sprinkle of determination, you can secure rewarding opportunities that align with your skills and passions.

Strategies for Finding Freelance Gigs:

1. Freelance Platforms: Websites like Upwork, Freelancer, and Fiverr connect freelancers with clients seeking various services. Create a compelling profile, showcase your skills, and actively apply for relevant gigs. Tailor your proposals to demonstrate how your expertise can solve the client's specific needs.

2. Networking: Leverage your professional network and social media platforms to connect with potential clients. Attend industry events, join online forums, and participate in relevant discussions. Personal connections often lead to valuable freelance opportunities.

3. Job Boards and Forums: Explore niche-specific job boards and forums related to your field. Many industries have dedicated platforms where businesses post freelance opportunities. Regularly check these platforms for new listings and respond promptly to job postings.

4. Cold Pitching: Identify businesses or individuals who could benefit from your services. Craft a personalized pitch outlining how your expertise can add value to their projects. Be concise, and persuasive, and highlight your unique selling points.

5. Content Marketing: Create valuable content related to your niche, such as blog posts, videos, or webinars. Content marketing establishes your expertise and attracts clients who appreciate your knowledge. Include a call-to-action in your content, inviting readers or viewers to hire you for further assistance.

Managing Client Relationships

Securing freelance gigs is just the beginning; maintaining positive client relationships is essential for long-term success. Happy clients not only lead to repeat business but also serve as valuable referrals and testimonials.

Effective Client Relationship Management:

1. Clear Communication: Establish open and transparent communication from the start. Clearly define project scopes, timelines, and expectations. Regularly update clients on your progress and be responsive to their queries and concerns.

2. Professionalism: Maintain a high level of professionalism in all interactions. Be punctual, meet deadlines, and deliver high-quality work. Address issues promptly and take responsibility for any mistakes, demonstrating your commitment to client satisfaction.

3. Active Listening: Listen carefully to your client's needs and preferences. Understanding their vision allows you to deliver tailored solutions. Ask questions to clarify uncertainties and ensure you're on the same page regarding project requirements.

4. Setting Boundaries: Clearly define your working hours, response times, and revision policies. Setting boundaries establishes mutual respect and prevents misunderstandings. Inform clients in advance if there are any changes to the project timeline or scope.

5. Exceeding Expectations: Go the extra mile to exceed client expectations. Surprise them with exceptional work quality, additional resources, or valuable insights. Over-delivering fosters trust and loyalty, encouraging clients to return for future projects.

6. Collecting Feedback: Regularly request feedback from clients upon project completion. Constructive criticism helps you improve your services, while positive feedback can be showcased in your portfolio and testimonials, enhancing your credibility.

Remember, freelance success isn't just about completing individual projects; it's about building lasting relationships that contribute to your reputation and business growth. By finding the right gigs and managing client relationships effectively, you'll establish yourself as a reliable and sought-after freelancer in your niche. Stay proactive, adaptable, and client-focused, and your freelance career will flourish.

Chapter 3

Dropshipping Deconstructed

Understanding Dropshipping

Dropshipping, a business model that has revolutionized the way entrepreneurs approach e-commerce, offers a low-risk, high-reward approach to selling products online. In this chapter, we'll delve into the fundamentals of dropshipping, uncovering the secrets behind its popularity and exploring how you can leverage this innovative model to build a profitable online store.

What Is Dropshipping?
Traditionally, running an e-commerce store meant investing in inventory, managing stock levels, and handling shipping logistics. Dropshipping, however, turns this conventional approach on its head. In dropshipping, you, as the store owner, don't hold any inventory. Instead, when a customer places an order on your website, the product is shipped directly from the supplier or manufacturer to the customer. This means you never have to deal with the hassles of inventory

management or shipping, allowing you to focus solely on sales and marketing.

The Advantages of Dropshipping:

1. Low Initial Investment: Since you don't need to purchase and store inventory upfront, the initial investment in dropshipping is significantly lower compared to traditional retail models. This makes it an attractive option for budding entrepreneurs with limited capital.

2. Flexibility and Scalability: With drop shipping, you can easily add or remove products from your online store without the constraints of physical inventory. This flexibility allows you to test various products and niches, scaling your business as demand grows.

3. Reduced Risk: Since you only purchase products after you've made a sale, there's no risk of being stuck with unsold inventory. Your business operates on a per-order basis, minimizing financial risks associated with surplus stock.

4. Focus on Marketing: Without the burden of inventory management, you can channel your energy and resources into marketing, customer service, and enhancing the overall shopping experience for your customers.

Finding the Right Products

In dropshipping, the products you choose to sell play a pivotal role in your store's success. Identifying the right products involves a careful blend of market research, trend analysis, and understanding your target audience's needs and preferences.

Steps to Finding Profitable Products:

1. Niche Selection: Focus on a specific niche or market segment. Niches allow you to target a particular audience with tailored products, making your marketing efforts more effective. Research niches with passionate communities and identifiable needs.

2. Market Research: Investigate trends, popular products, and emerging markets. Use tools like Google Trends, social media platforms, and e-commerce marketplaces to identify products that are gaining traction. Analyze competitors within your chosen niche to understand their best-selling items.

3. Product Quality and Reliability: Partner with reputable suppliers who offer high-quality products and reliable shipping services. Customer satisfaction is paramount in dropshipping; selling inferior or unreliable products can tarnish your reputation.

4. Profit Margin Analysis: Calculate your potential profit margins by considering product costs, shipping fees, and other expenses. Aim for products with a healthy profit margin that allows you to cover your operational costs and invest in marketing efforts.

5. Seasonal Considerations: Be mindful of seasonal trends and products. Some items might experience high demand during specific times of the year, such as holidays or special events. Plan your product offerings around these seasons to capitalize on increased demand.

6. Unique Selling Proposition (USP): Consider what sets your products apart from competitors. It could be superior quality, unique features, or exceptional customer service. Highlight your USP in your marketing efforts to attract customers looking for something special.

Understanding the essence of dropshipping and strategically selecting the right products are the building blocks of a successful dropshipping venture. By grasping the nuances of this business model and conducting thorough product research, you position yourself to create a thriving online store that caters to your customers' desires while maximizing your profits. Stay innovative, stay informed, and you'll unlock the full potential of dropshipping.

Setting Up Your Dropshipping Store

Setting up your dropshipping store is a pivotal step that requires meticulous planning and attention to detail. In this section, we'll guide you through the essential elements of creating a professional, user-friendly online store that not only captivates visitors but also converts them into loyal customers.

1. Choosing the Right E-Commerce Platform:
Selecting the right platform is fundamental to your dropshipping success. Popular platforms like Shopify, WooCommerce (for WordPress), and BigCommerce offer user-friendly interfaces, customizable templates, and integrations with dropshipping apps. Evaluate each platform based on your specific needs, budget, and technical expertise.

2. Designing a User-Friendly Website:

Clean and Intuitive Layout: Ensure your website is easy to navigate. Use clear menus, logical categorization, and intuitive user interfaces to guide visitors seamlessly through your products.

Mobile Optimization: With a growing number of users accessing websites via smartphones, your site must be mobile-responsive. Optimize images and content for various screen sizes to enhance the user experience.

High-Quality Visuals: Invest in high-quality product images and videos. Visuals play a significant role in online purchasing decisions. Include multiple images, allowing customers to view products from different angles.

3. Integrating Dropshipping Suppliers:

Partner with reliable dropshipping suppliers who offer a wide range of products, competitive pricing, and efficient shipping services. Integrate your chosen suppliers with your e-commerce platform using dropshipping apps or plugins. Automated order processing ensures seamless transactions between your store and the supplier.

4. Implementing Secure Payment Gateways:

Select trustworthy payment gateways to process transactions securely. Offer multiple payment options, including credit/debit cards, PayPal, and digital wallets, to cater to diverse customer preferences. A secure checkout process instills confidence in your customers, reducing cart abandonment rates.

5. Setting Up Customer Support:

Provide excellent customer support to enhance your store's reputation. Offer multiple communication channels, such as live chat, email, and phone support. Address customer inquiries promptly, resolve issues professionally, and maintain a positive and helpful demeanor.

Marketing and Sales Strategies

With your dropshipping store in place, it's time to focus on marketing and sales strategies that drive traffic, engage visitors, and convert them into paying customers.

1. Search Engine Optimization (SEO):
Optimize your website for search engines to increase organic traffic. Conduct keyword research to identify relevant search terms within your niche. Incorporate these keywords into product descriptions, meta titles, and headings. Focus on creating high-quality, informative content that adds value to your audience.

2. Social Media Marketing:
Leverage social media platforms to build brand awareness and engage with potential customers. Identify the platforms where your target audience is most active and create compelling content, including product showcases, tutorials, and customer testimonials. Encourage social sharing and interaction to expand your reach.

3. Pay-Per-Click (PPC) Advertising:
Invest in paid advertising campaigns, such as Google Ads or Facebook Ads, to target specific demographics and promote your products. Create visually appealing ads with concise, persuasive copy. Monitor campaign

performance, analyze data, and refine your strategies to maximize return on investment (ROI).

4. Email Marketing:
Build an email list of interested prospects and customers. Send targeted email campaigns, including product updates, promotions, and exclusive offers. Personalize messages based on customer preferences and behavior to increase engagement. Implement email automation to nurture leads and encourage repeat purchases.

5. Influencer Marketing:
Collaborate with influencers and bloggers within your niche. Influencers can showcase your products to their followers, providing authentic reviews and testimonials. Partner with influencers whose audience aligns with your target demographic for maximum impact.

6. Customer Retention Strategies:
Encourage customer loyalty by offering loyalty programs, discounts on future purchases, and personalized recommendations based on past buying behavior. Request feedback from customers and actively address their suggestions and concerns. A satisfied customer is more likely to become a repeat buyer and recommend your store to others.

By implementing these comprehensive strategies, you'll create a powerful synergy between your dropshipping store setup and your marketing efforts. Stay agile, adapt to market trends, and continuously analyze your results to refine your approach. With dedication, creativity, and a customer-centric mindset, you'll not only drive traffic to your store but also foster meaningful relationships with your customers, ensuring the sustained success of your dropshipping business.

Chapter 4

E-Commerce Essentials

Setting Up an Online Store

Your e-commerce store is your digital shopfront, the place where visitors become customers. In this section, we'll explore the foundational aspects of establishing an online store that not only attracts potential buyers but also provides a seamless and trustworthy shopping experience.

Choosing the Right E-Commerce Platform:
Selecting the right e-commerce platform is a critical decision. It affects everything from design and functionality to payment processing and scalability. Popular platforms like Shopify, WooCommerce, and BigCommerce offer user-friendly interfaces, customizable templates, and robust features to suit various business sizes and models. Consider the following when choosing a platform:

Ease of Use: How comfortable are you with the platform's interface? Is it intuitive, and does it align with your technical skill level?

Customization: Can you tailor the design to match your brand and offer a unique shopping experience?

Scalability: Does the platform accommodate your business growth? It should be able to handle an increase in traffic and sales volume.

Integration: Look for seamless integration with payment gateways, shipping solutions, and third-party tools for analytics and marketing.

Designing a User-Friendly Online Store:

Clean Layout: Create a visually appealing layout with clear navigation, product categories, and a user-friendly search bar.

Mobile Optimization: Ensure your store is mobile-responsive to accommodate users on various devices.

High-Quality Product Images: Invest in high-resolution images and videos to showcase your products. Include multiple images from different angles to provide a comprehensive view.

Product Descriptions: Craft detailed and persuasive product descriptions that highlight features, benefits, and unique selling points.

Easy Checkout Process: Simplify the checkout process with minimal steps, guest checkout options, and multiple payment methods.

Security and Trust Signals: Display trust signals such as SSL certificates and secure payment icons to reassure customers about the safety of their transactions.

Product Sourcing and Inventory Management

Efficient product sourcing and inventory management are essential for running a successful e-commerce operation.

1. Product Sourcing:

Dropshipping: If you've chosen the dropshipping model, establish relationships with reliable suppliers. Ensure they offer a wide range of products, competitive pricing, and dependable shipping services.

Wholesale or Manufacturer Direct: If you decide to stock your own inventory, source products from wholesalers or directly from manufacturers. Consider factors such as minimum order quantities, lead times, and quality.

2. Inventory Management:

Inventory Tracking: Implement inventory management software or tools to track stock levels, monitor sales, and receive alerts for low-stock items.

Product Organization: Categorize products logically and create a system for easy access. Consider implementing a barcode or SKU system for efficient tracking.

Seasonal and Trend Analysis: Stay attuned to market trends and seasonal demand fluctuations. Adjust your inventory accordingly to avoid overstocking or understocking.

Quality Control: Regularly inspect incoming inventory to ensure product quality. Return or replace damaged or defective items promptly.

Order Fulfillment: Streamline your order fulfillment process, including picking, packing, and shipping. Efficient fulfillment leads to faster delivery and increased customer satisfaction.

By setting up an online store that's visually appealing and user-friendly, and by implementing effective inventory management practices, you'll create a strong foundation for your e-commerce business. Your digital shopfront should inspire trust, offer a seamless shopping experience, and provide an organized and efficient system for product sourcing and inventory control. Keep refining your e-commerce store's operations to adapt to changing market dynamics and customer expectations, and you'll be well on your way to e-commerce success.

Website Optimization and User Experience

A seamless user experience is at the heart of a successful e-commerce venture. In this section, we'll explore website optimization techniques and strategies to enhance user experience, ensuring that visitors not only find your online store but also stay engaged and make purchases.

Website Optimization:

1. Page Speed Optimization: Slow-loading pages can deter visitors. Optimize images, use efficient coding practices, and leverage caching mechanisms to improve page load times.

2. Mobile-Friendly Design: With a growing number of users accessing websites via smartphones and tablets, ensure your site is mobile-responsive. Test your site's functionality across various devices to guarantee a consistent experience.

3. Intuitive Navigation: Design a clear and intuitive menu structure. Use logical categorization and product filters to help visitors find what they're looking for easily.

4. Streamlined Checkout Process: Simplify the checkout process by minimizing the number of steps required. Offer guest checkout options and provide clear instructions at each stage of the transaction.

5. Security Measures: Implement SSL encryption to secure customer data. Display trust badges and secure payment icons to instill confidence in visitors.

6. Optimized Product Pages: Each product page should have high-quality images, compelling descriptions, clear pricing, and prominent call-to-action buttons. Include customer reviews and ratings to enhance trust.

User Experience Enhancement:

1. Personalization: Use data to personalize user experiences. Recommend products based on past purchases or browsing history. Personalized product recommendations can significantly boost sales.

2. Live Chat Support: Implement live chat functionality to provide instant assistance to customers. Addressing queries in real time can improve customer satisfaction and increase conversions.

3. User-Generated Content: Encourage customers to leave reviews, share photos of their purchases, or create unboxing videos. User-generated content adds authenticity and credibility to your products.

4. A/B Testing: Conduct A/B tests on various elements of your website, such as call-to-action buttons, color schemes, or product layouts. Analyze the results to optimize for higher conversions.

5. **Loading Error Management:** Customize error messages to guide users effectively if they encounter page not found or other errors. Provide clear navigation options to keep them engaged.

Marketing Your E-Commerce Business

Marketing your e-commerce business is essential to attract potential customers, drive sales, and foster brand loyalty. Let's explore effective marketing strategies to increase your online store's visibility and profitability.

1. Search Engine Optimization (SEO):

Keyword Research: Identify relevant keywords within your niche. Optimize product titles, descriptions, and meta tags to improve search engine rankings.

Content Marketing: Create high-quality blog posts, videos, and guides related to your products or industry. Content marketing not only attracts organic traffic but also establishes your authority in the field.

2. Social Media Marketing:

Platform Selection: Choose social media platforms based on your target audience. For visual products, platforms like Instagram and Pinterest can be highly effective.

Engagement: Regularly post engaging content, respond to comments, and interact with your audience. Social media platforms are ideal for building a community around your brand.

3. Pay-Per-Click (PPC) Advertising:

Google Ads: Run Google Ads campaigns to target potential customers actively searching for your products. Use compelling ad copy and relevant keywords for optimal results.

Social Media Ads: Leverage social media advertising to reach specific demographics. Facebook and Instagram offer detailed targeting options to tailor your ads to the right audience.

4. Email Marketing:

Email Sequences: Set up automated email sequences for welcome emails, abandoned cart reminders, and post-purchase follow-ups. Personalize emails based on customer behavior and preferences.

Promotional Campaigns: Send newsletters with exclusive offers, new product launches, or seasonal discounts to incentivize purchases.

5. Influencer Marketing:

Influencer Partnerships: Collaborate with influencers whose audience aligns with your target demographic. Influencers can create authentic content showcasing your products to their followers.

Affiliate Marketing: Implement an affiliate marketing program where partners earn a commission for every sale they generate through their referrals.

By optimizing your website for a seamless user experience and implementing diverse marketing strategies, you'll create a powerful online presence and attract a steady stream of potential customers. Stay adaptable, continuously analyze your efforts, and be willing to adjust your strategies based on customer feedback and market trends. With a user-friendly website and effective marketing techniques, your e-commerce business will thrive, driving both growth and customer satisfaction.

Stay adaptable, continuously analyze your efforts, and be willing to adjust your strategies based on customer feedback and market trends.

Chapter 5

The 30-Day Action Plan

Week 1: Preparation and Planning

Embarking on your 30-day journey to start a side hustle is an exciting endeavor. The first week is all about laying a strong foundation, clarifying your goals, and setting up the necessary groundwork for a successful side hustle. Let's break down the key tasks and actions for Week 1.

Day 1-2: Define Your Side Hustle Idea

1. Brainstorm Ideas: Reflect on your passions, skills, and interests. Identify potential side hustle ideas that align with your strengths and market demand.

2. Market Research: Conduct initial research on your chosen ideas. Analyze competitors, target audience, and potential profitability. Identify gaps in the market and areas where you can add unique value.

3. Choose Your Niche: Narrow down your ideas to a specific niche. Focus on a niche that excites you, has a viable market, and allows room for growth.

Day 3-4: Set Clear Goals and Objectives

1. SMART Goals: Define your goals using the SMART criteria (Specific, Measurable, Achievable, Relevant, Time-bound). For example, set a goal like "Earn $500 in the first month by selling handmade crafts online."

2. Break Down Tasks: Divide your goals into smaller, actionable tasks. Create a list of tasks you need to accomplish to achieve your goals, both short-term and long-term.

Day 5-7: Create Your Business Plan

1. Executive Summary: Write a brief overview of your side hustle, outlining your mission, target audience, and unique selling proposition.

2. Market Analysis: Conduct a detailed analysis of your niche and target market. Identify competitors, market trends, and potential challenges.

3. Business Model: Decide on your side hustle model (freelancing, dropshipping, e-commerce, etc.) and outline the revenue streams, pricing strategy, and customer acquisition plan.

4. Financial Projections: Create a basic financial forecast for the first month. Estimate your expenses, potential revenue, and profit margins. This will give you an initial idea of your financial viability.

5. Action Plan: Develop a detailed action plan for the next 30 days. Break down tasks week by week, setting specific deadlines for each task. Be realistic about what you can accomplish within the given time frame.

End of Week 1: Reflect and Refine

Take some time to reflect on your progress during the first week. Review your business plan, goals, and tasks. Make any necessary adjustments based on your initial research and planning. Stay focused, stay motivated, and get ready to dive into Week 2, where you'll start putting your plans into action and bringing your side hustle to life. Remember, consistency, dedication, and adaptability are key to your success!

Week 2: Building Your Online Presence

Congratulations on completing the first week of your 30-day action plan! Now, it's time to take your side hustle to the next level by establishing a strong online presence. This week, you'll focus on creating a professional brand identity, building your website, and setting up your social media presence.

Day 1-2: Define Your Brand Identity

1. Brand Name: Choose a unique and memorable name for your side hustle. Ensure the name is available as a domain if you plan to create a website.

2. Logo and Visuals: Design a professional logo and select a cohesive color scheme and typography. Consistent visuals create a strong brand identity.

3. Brand Story: Craft a compelling story about your side hustle. Explain your mission, values, and what sets your business apart. Storytelling connects with customers on a personal level.

Day 3-4: Create Your Website

1. Domain and Hosting: Register your domain name and choose a reliable hosting provider. Platforms like

Shopify, WordPress (with WooCommerce), or Wix offer user-friendly website-building tools.

2. Website Design: Customize your website template to align with your brand identity. Ensure a clean layout, intuitive navigation, and mobile responsiveness.

3. Essential Pages: Create essential pages like Home, About Us, Products/Services, Contact, and a Blog (if applicable). Provide clear and concise information on each page.

4. Product/Service Listings: If you're selling products, add detailed product listings with high-quality images, descriptions, and prices. For services, clearly outline what you offer, pricing, and how customers can contact you.

Day 5-6: Set Up Social Media Profiles

1. Choose Platforms: Determine which social media platforms are most relevant to your audience. Consider platforms like Facebook, Instagram, Twitter, LinkedIn, or Pinterest based on your niche.

2. Profile Optimization: Complete your profiles with your brand logo, a compelling bio, and a link to your website. Consistent branding across platforms is key.

3. Content Strategy: Plan your content strategy. Decide what type of content you'll share, how often, and the tone of your posts. Create a content calendar to stay organized.

Day 7: Engage Your Audience

1. First Post: Make your first social media post introducing your side hustle. Share your brand story, what you offer, and how it benefits your customers.

2. Engage with Others: Interact with relevant posts from others in your niche. Engaging with the community helps you connect with potential customers and collaborators.

3. Collect Feedback: Encourage friends, family, or early followers to provide feedback on your website and social media profiles. Use their input to make necessary improvements.

End of Week 2: Reflect and Refine Your Online Presence

At the end of the week, evaluate your website and social media profiles. Ensure your branding is consistent, and your messaging is clear and engaging. Be responsive to any feedback received and make necessary adjustments. With a professional website and active social media presence, you're now ready to move on to Week 3, where you'll focus on marketing strategies to attract your first customers. Stay enthusiastic, stay adaptable, and keep building your dream side hustle!

Week 3: Attracting Your First Customers

Welcome to Week 3 of your 30-day action plan! This week is all about attracting your first customers and driving initial sales. With your online presence established, it's time to implement targeted marketing strategies and engage with your audience effectively.

Day 1-2: Launch Your Marketing Campaigns

1. Social Media Marketing: Create engaging social media posts showcasing your products/services. Use eye-catching visuals, compelling captions, and relevant hashtags. Encourage followers to share your posts.

2. Email Marketing: If you've collected email addresses, send out a launch email to your subscribers. Offer an exclusive promotion or early access to incentivize purchases.

3. Paid Advertising: Consider running targeted ads on social media platforms or Google Ads. Set a budget, define your audience, and create compelling ad copy and visuals.

Day 3-4: Collaborate and Network

1. Influencer Collaborations: Reach out to influencers or bloggers in your niche. Collaborate with them to promote your products/services to their audience. Influencer testimonials can boost credibility.

2. Partnerships: Identify potential partners or complementary businesses. Collaborate on joint promotions or cross-promotions. Partnerships can expand your reach to a wider audience.

Day 5-6: Engage with Your Audience

1. Customer Engagement: Respond promptly to customer inquiries and comments on social media and your website. Engage with your audience by asking questions, running polls, and encouraging discussions.

2. User-Generated Content: Encourage customers to share their experiences with your products/services. User-generated content, such as reviews and testimonials, builds trust and authenticity.

Day 7: Analyze and Adjust

1. Performance Analysis: Review the performance of your marketing campaigns. Track metrics like website visits, click-through rates, and conversion rates. Identify which channels and strategies are generating the most traffic and sales.

2. Customer Feedback: Collect feedback from customers who made purchases. Understand their experience, what they liked, and areas for improvement. Use this feedback to enhance your products/services and customer service.

3. Iterate Your Strategies: Based on your analysis, refine your marketing strategies. Allocate more resources to the most effective channels and adjust your messaging to better resonate with your audience.

End of Week 3: Reflect and Plan for Growth
As you conclude Week 3, celebrate your achievements and the customers you've attracted. Take time to analyze what worked well and what needs improvement. Use this insight to plan your strategies for the coming weeks and months.

Remember, building a customer base takes time and persistence. Stay consistent in your efforts, remain responsive to customer needs, and continue refining your marketing tactics. With dedication and a customer-focused approach, you're well on your way to building a thriving side hustle.

Week 4: Scaling and Growth

Congratulations on reaching Week 4 of your 30-day action plan! This week marks a pivotal moment in your side hustle journey, as you shift your focus from initial customer acquisition to scaling your business and laying the foundation for sustainable growth. Let's dive into the strategies you can implement to scale your side hustle and prepare for long-term success.

Day 1-2: Analyze Your Performance

1. Sales and Revenue Analysis: Review your sales data from the past weeks. Identify your best-selling products or services, highest revenue-generating channels, and customer demographics. Use this information to refine your offerings and marketing strategies.

2. Customer Feedback Review: Reflect on the feedback received from customers. Identify recurring themes or suggestions for improvement. Address any negative feedback and use positive feedback to reinforce your strengths.

Day 3-4: Optimize Your Operations

1. Efficient Order Fulfillment: Streamline your order fulfillment process. Ensure prompt shipping, accurate packaging, and clear communication with customers regarding their orders. Consider implementing automated systems to handle routine tasks.

2. Inventory Management: Fine-tune your inventory management strategies. Monitor stock levels, identify fast-moving products, and replenish inventory to avoid stockouts. Explore bulk purchasing or negotiating better deals with suppliers to optimize costs.

Day 5-6: Enhance Customer Experience

1. Exceptional Customer Service: Provide exceptional customer service to build customer loyalty. Address inquiries promptly, handle complaints professionally, and go the extra mile to exceed customer expectations.

2. Personalization: Implement personalization techniques in your marketing and customer interactions. Use customer data to tailor product recommendations, marketing messages, and special offers to individual preferences.

Day 7: Develop Long-Term Growth Strategies

1. Diversification: Explore opportunities to diversify your product or service offerings. Consider expanding into related niches or introducing complementary products to cater to a broader customer base.

2. Marketing Expansion: Expand your marketing efforts to new channels or demographics. Experiment with different advertising platforms, social media channels, or content formats. Test and analyze the performance of these experiments to identify successful avenues.

3. Customer Retention: Implement customer retention strategies, such as loyalty programs, subscription services, or exclusive member benefits. Repeat customers are often more valuable and cost-effective to your business.

End of Week 4: Celebrate Your Achievements and Plan Ahead

As you conclude Week 4, take a moment to celebrate your achievements and the progress you've made. You've successfully launched your side hustle, attracted your first customers, and laid the foundation for growth. Reflect on the lessons learned, challenges overcome, and the valuable experience gained.

Looking ahead, continue to adapt, innovate, and refine your strategies. Stay informed about market trends, listen to your customers, and be open to feedback. Keep nurturing your relationships with customers, suppliers, and partners.

Remember, the journey of entrepreneurship is continuous. Embrace the challenges, celebrate the successes, and keep pushing your boundaries. With determination, creativity, and a customer-centric approach, your side hustle has the potential to grow into a thriving and sustainable business. Best of luck on your entrepreneurial journey!

Chapter 6

Financial Management

Budgeting and Expenses

Effective financial management is essential for the success and sustainability of your side hustle. In this chapter, we'll explore key aspects of financial management, including budgeting, tracking expenses, and developing pricing strategies.

Budgeting for Your Side Hustle:

1. Start with a Clear Budget: Outline your income and expenses. Determine how much you can allocate to different areas of your business, such as marketing, product sourcing, and operational costs.

2. Fixed vs. Variable Expenses: Differentiate between fixed expenses (constant, regular payments like subscriptions) and variable expenses (costs that fluctuate, like raw materials). Prioritize fixed expenses and allocate the remaining budget to variable costs.

3. Emergency Fund: Set aside a portion of your earnings as an emergency fund. This fund acts as a financial safety net, providing stability during unexpected expenses or low sales periods.

Tracking Expenses:

1. Expense Categories: Categorize your expenses into different groups, such as materials, marketing, packaging, and operational costs. Detailed categorization helps you identify areas where you can optimize spending.

2. Expense Tracking Tools: Use accounting software or expense tracking apps to monitor your expenditures. These tools automate the process, provide real-time insights, and simplify financial record-keeping.

3. Regular Audits: Conduct regular expense audits to identify unnecessary costs or areas where you can cut expenses. Negotiate with suppliers for better rates and explore cost-effective alternatives without compromising quality.

Pricing Strategies

1. Cost-Based Pricing: Calculate the total cost of producing your product or delivering your service. Add a profit margin to determine the selling price. Consider factors like labor, materials, overhead, and desired profit.

2. Market-Based Pricing: Research competitors' prices and market demand. Set your prices competitively, taking into account the value you offer compared to competitors. Adjust your prices based on market trends and customer preferences.

3. Value-Based Pricing: Determine the value your product or service provides to customers. Price your offerings based on the perceived value to the customer rather than solely on production costs. Premium quality, unique features, or exceptional customer service can justify higher prices.

4. Dynamic Pricing: For online businesses, consider dynamic pricing strategies that adjust prices based on demand, customer behavior, or market conditions. Implement algorithms that optimize prices for maximum profitability.

Financial Health and Growth:

1. Profit Reinvestment: Reinvest a portion of your profits back into the business. Allocate funds for marketing campaigns, product expansion, or process improvements to drive growth.

2. Regular Financial Check-Ins: Schedule regular financial check-ins to assess your financial health. Review profit and loss statements, cash flow, and budget adherence. Use these insights to make informed decisions about your business.

3. Professional Financial Advice: Consider consulting with a financial advisor or accountant, especially as your side hustle grows. Professional advice can help you navigate complex financial decisions and optimize your business's financial health.

By mastering budgeting, tracking expenses, and implementing strategic pricing, you'll build a solid financial foundation for your side hustle. Effective financial management not only ensures your business's stability but also positions you for sustainable growth and long-term success. Stay vigilant, adapt to changing market conditions, and always prioritize the financial health of your side hustle.

Managing Cash Flow

Cash flow management is vital for the smooth operation of your side hustle. Proper management ensures you can cover operational expenses, invest in growth, and handle unexpected costs. Here's how you can effectively manage your cash flow:

1. Cash Flow Forecasting:

Predict Income and Expenses: Estimate your monthly income and list all expected expenses. This includes production costs, marketing expenses, utilities, and any other overheads.

Identify Cash Gaps: Anticipate periods where your expenses might exceed your income. Prepare for these gaps by having an emergency fund or a line of credit as a financial cushion.

2. Invoicing and Payment Terms:

Clear Invoicing: Send professional, detailed invoices promptly after completing a sale or service. Clearly outline payment terms, due dates, and any late fees.

Optimize Payment Terms: Negotiate payment terms with suppliers and consider offering discounts for early payments from clients to improve your cash flow.

3. Inventory Management:

Just-in-Time Inventory: Adopt a just-in-time inventory system to minimize excess stock. This approach reduces storage costs and ensures you're not tying up cash in unsold products.

Monitor Stock Levels: Regularly assess your inventory to avoid overstocking items that might become obsolete.

4. Expenses Control:

Cost-Effective Decisions: Evaluate all expenses critically. Look for cost-effective alternatives without compromising quality.

Regular Expense Audits: Periodically review your expenses to identify areas for optimization. Cut unnecessary costs and renegotiate contracts when possible.

Tax Considerations for Side Hustlers

1. Separate Business and Personal Finances:

Dedicated Accounts: Open a separate business bank account to keep business finances distinct from personal finances. This simplifies tax reporting and ensures accurate financial records.

2. Understand Tax Obligations:

Tax Classification: Determine your business structure (sole proprietorship, LLC, etc.) as it affects how you report income and expenses.

Estimated Taxes: Since side hustlers are typically self-employed, you may need to pay estimated quarterly taxes. Consult a tax professional to calculate these payments accurately.

3. Keep Detailed Records:

Receipts and Invoices: Keep thorough records of all receipts, invoices, and expenses. Digital record-keeping platforms can help organize your financial documents.

4. Deductions and Credits:

Tax Deductions: Familiarize yourself with business-related tax deductions. Common deductions include home office expenses, mileage, supplies, and marketing costs.

Tax Credits: Explore potential tax credits applicable to your business, such as those for research and development or renewable energy use.

5. Consult a Tax Professional:

Professional Guidance: Consider consulting a tax professional or accountant familiar with small businesses and side hustles. They can provide tailored advice, ensuring you take advantage of applicable tax benefits and comply with regulations.

By managing cash flow effectively and understanding your tax obligations, you safeguard your side hustle against financial pitfalls and legal complications. Stay proactive, stay informed, and seek professional guidance when needed to maintain a strong financial foundation for your business.

Chapter 7

Time Management and Work-Life Balance

Organizing Your Schedule

Time management is crucial for balancing your side hustle with other aspects of your life and ensuring optimal productivity. In this chapter, we'll explore effective time management strategies and how to organize your schedule for a harmonious work-life balance.

Organizing Your Schedule:

1. Set Clear Goals: Define specific, measurable goals for your side hustle. Break them down into smaller tasks and prioritize them based on importance and deadlines.

2. Create a Daily Routine: Establish a daily routine that incorporates dedicated time for your side hustle. Consistency helps train your mind to focus during these periods, increasing productivity.

3. Time Blocking: Allocate specific blocks of time for different tasks or categories of work. Designate focused periods for tasks like marketing, product development, and customer service. Avoid multitasking, as it can lead to decreased efficiency.

4. Use Productivity Techniques: Implement techniques like the Pomodoro Technique (working in short bursts with breaks) or the Eisenhower Matrix (prioritizing tasks based on urgency and importance) to enhance focus and efficiency.

5. Utilize Tools and Apps: Leverage productivity tools and apps, such as calendars, to-do lists, and project management software. These tools can help you organize tasks, set reminders, and track your progress.

Managing Your Work-Life Balance:

1. Set Boundaries: Clearly define your working hours and communicate them to friends, family, and clients. Establishing boundaries ensures uninterrupted work periods and designated relaxation time.

2. Schedule Breaks: Factor in regular breaks during your work hours. Short breaks enhance focus and prevent burnout. Use this time to stretch, take a walk, or engage in activities that relax your mind.

3. Prioritize Self-Care: Allocate time for self-care activities, such as exercise, hobbies, and spending quality time with loved ones. Taking care of your physical and mental well-being is essential for sustained productivity.

4. Learn to Say No: Don't overcommit yourself. Assess your capacity realistically and decline additional tasks or projects if they threaten your work-life balance. Quality work is more important than quantity.

5. Practice Mindfulness: Incorporate mindfulness practices, such as meditation or deep breathing, into your routine. These exercises can reduce stress, enhance focus, and improve overall well-being.

Evaluate and Adjust:

1. Regular Assessment: Periodically evaluate your time management strategies and work-life balance. Assess what's working well and what needs improvement. Be adaptable and willing to make adjustments based on your experiences.

2. Celebrate Achievements: Acknowledge your achievements and milestones. Celebrating your successes, no matter how small boosts motivation and encourages continued dedication to your side hustle.

3. Seek Support: If you find it challenging to manage your time effectively or struggle with work-life balance, consider seeking support from a mentor, coach, or support group. Learning from others' experiences can provide valuable insights.

By organizing your schedule effectively, setting clear boundaries, and maintaining a healthy work-life balance, you'll not only maximize your productivity but also ensure your overall well-being. Remember that achieving a balance that works for you might require experimentation and adjustment. Stay mindful, stay organized, and nurture both your side hustle and your personal life to create a fulfilling and sustainable lifestyle.

Avoiding Burnout

Avoiding burnout is crucial when managing a side hustle alongside other responsibilities. Burnout can drain your enthusiasm, creativity, and overall energy. Here's how you can prevent burnout and sustain your passion for your side hustle:

1. Set Realistic Expectations:

Manageable Goals: Establish achievable goals and deadlines. Avoid setting unrealistic expectations that could lead to excessive stress and frustration.

Celebrate Progress: Acknowledge and celebrate your achievements, no matter how small. Recognizing your progress boosts morale and motivation.

2. Learn to Delegate:

Outsource Tasks: Identify tasks that can be outsourced or delegated. Hiring freelancers or seeking assistance from friends and family for specific tasks can lighten your workload.

Focus on Strengths: Concentrate on tasks that align with your skills and passions. Delegate tasks that are outside your expertise to individuals who can handle them effectively.

3. Practice Self-Care:

Rest and Recovery: Ensure you get adequate sleep, exercise regularly, and take breaks. Prioritize activities that relax and rejuvenate you.

Mindfulness and Relaxation: Engage in mindfulness activities like meditation or hobbies that bring you joy. Allocate time for activities that promote mental well-being.

4. Learn to Say No:

Prioritize Commitments: Evaluate your commitments and learn to decline additional tasks or projects that may overwhelm you. It's okay to decline opportunities if they strain your resources.

Balancing Your Side Hustle with Your Full-Time Job

1. Time Blocking and Prioritization:

Structured Schedule: Use time blocking to allocate specific hours to your side hustle and your full-time job. Clearly define working hours for each role to avoid overlapping responsibilities.

Priority Tasks: Identify high-priority tasks in both your side hustle and full-time job. Allocate focused time to complete these tasks effectively.

2. Communicate Effectively:

Transparent Communication: Be transparent with your employer and colleagues about your side hustle. If possible, negotiate a flexible schedule or remote work options to accommodate both commitments.

Set Boundaries: Clearly define your availability for work-related tasks and side hustle responsibilities. Set boundaries to prevent one role from encroaching on the other.

3. Manage Energy Levels:

Optimize Productivity: Identify your peak energy periods during the day. Schedule demanding tasks during these times to maximize productivity.

Rest and Recharge: Ensure you allocate time for relaxation and social activities outside work. Social connections and downtime are essential for mental and emotional well-being.

4. Seek Support and Mentorship:

Supportive Network: Surround yourself with supportive friends, family, and mentors who understand your commitments. They can offer guidance, encouragement, and practical help.

Mentorship: Seek mentorship from individuals who have successfully balanced side hustles and full-time jobs. Learning from their experiences can provide valuable insights.

Balancing a side hustle with a full-time job is demanding, but with effective time management, clear communication, and self-care practices, it is entirely achievable. Remember, it's essential to listen to your body and mind. If you feel overwhelmed, don't hesitate to seek professional help or adjust your commitments accordingly. With the right strategies and a supportive network, you can successfully manage both roles while maintaining your well-being and enthusiasm.

Chapter 8

Overcoming Challenges

Dealing with Rejection and Failure

Every side hustle journey comes with its set of challenges. Overcoming these hurdles not only strengthens your business but also builds resilience and adaptability.

1. Stay Solution-Oriented:

Problem-Solving Mindset: Approach challenges with a problem-solving mindset. Instead of dwelling on the problem, focus on finding viable solutions. Break down complex issues into manageable tasks.

2. Learn from Setbacks:

Analytical Approach: Analyze the situation objectively. Identify the factors that led to the setback and evaluate the decisions made. Use failures as learning opportunities to refine your strategies and decision-making process.

3. Seek Guidance and Support:

Mentorship: Connect with mentors, experienced entrepreneurs, or industry experts. Their insights and advice can provide valuable perspectives and guidance in challenging situations.

Peer Support: Engage with fellow entrepreneurs or join support groups. Sharing experiences with others who have faced similar challenges can offer emotional support and practical solutions.

4. Embrace Adaptability:

Flexibility: Be open to adapting your strategies based on feedback and changing market conditions. A willingness to pivot and adjust your approach can help you overcome obstacles effectively.

Innovation: Encourage innovation within your side hustle. Explore new ideas, products, or services. Innovation can lead to differentiation and provide solutions to existing challenges.

5. Managing Finances:

Financial Planning: Maintain a healthy financial reserve to cushion your business during lean periods. Proper financial planning can help you navigate financial challenges with stability.

Expense Management: Regularly assess your expenses and cut down on non-essential costs. Efficient financial management ensures your resources are utilized effectively.

Dealing with Rejection and Failure: Turning Setbacks into Success

Rejection and failure are integral parts of entrepreneurship. How you handle these setbacks can determine your future success. Here are strategies to cope with rejection and turn failures into opportunities:

1. Embrace a Growth Mindset:

Continuous Learning: View failures as opportunities for growth. Embrace the mindset that failures are temporary setbacks and valuable lessons for future success.

Self-Reflection: Reflect on your experiences, acknowledging your mistakes without self-blame. Understand the factors contributing to the rejection and use this understanding to improve.

2. Persistence and Resilience:

Perseverance: Stay persistent in the face of rejection. Many successful entrepreneurs faced multiple rejections before achieving breakthroughs. Your determination can lead to eventual acceptance and success.

Resilience: Develop resilience to bounce back from failures. Cultivate a strong support system, practice self-care, and maintain a positive mindset to cope with setbacks effectively.

3. Turn Rejections into Opportunities:

Feedback Utilization: Seek feedback from rejections and use it constructively. Adapt your approach based on feedback to increase your chances of acceptance in the future.

Networking: Build and nurture relationships with industry professionals. Networking can create new opportunities and increase your visibility, potentially leading to positive outcomes.

4. Celebrate Small Wins:

Acknowledge Progress: Celebrate even the smallest victories. Acknowledging your progress, no matter how minor, boosts morale and motivates you to continue despite setbacks.

5. Practice Self-Compassion:

Self-Kindness: Be kind to yourself during times of rejection or failure. Avoid self-criticism and negative self-talk. Treat yourself with the same kindness and understanding you would offer a friend facing a similar situation.

Remember, challenges, rejections, and failures are not indicators of your worth or potential. They are natural aspects of the entrepreneurial journey.

Adapting to Market Changes

The business landscape is ever-changing, and successful side hustlers must adapt to market shifts to remain relevant and competitive. Here's how you can navigate market changes effectively:

1. Continuous Market Research:

Stay Informed: Regularly conduct market research to identify emerging trends, changing customer preferences, and new technologies. Staying informed helps you anticipate shifts in demand and adapt your offerings accordingly.

2. Flexibility and Innovation:

Be Flexible: Embrace flexibility in your business model. Be willing to pivot, modify your products or services, or explore new niches based on market demands. Adaptability is key to survival in a dynamic market.

Encourage Innovation: Foster a culture of innovation within your side hustle. Encourage your team (if applicable) or yourself to brainstorm new ideas and explore creative solutions to meet evolving market needs.

3. Customer Feedback and Engagement:

Listen to Customers: Actively seek feedback from your customers. Understand their pain points, preferences, and expectations. Use this feedback to refine your offerings and enhance customer satisfaction.

Engage with Customers: Build a strong relationship with your customers. Engage with them through social media, surveys, or direct communication. A loyal customer base can provide valuable insights and support during market shifts.

4. Diversify Revenue Streams:

Explore New Revenue Streams: Look for opportunities to diversify your income sources. Explore complementary products, services, or collaborations that align with your brand and can generate additional revenue.

Balance Dependency: Avoid over-reliance on a single product or service. Diversification spreads the risk and ensures your side hustle remains resilient even if one aspect of your business faces challenges.

Staying Motivated

Maintaining motivation and enthusiasm is essential for the long-term success of your side hustle. Here are strategies to keep your motivation levels high:

1. Revisit Your Why:
Clarify Your Purpose: Reconnect with your initial motivation for starting the side hustle. Clarify your purpose, goals, and the impact you want to create. A clear sense of purpose fuels motivation.

2. Set Milestones and Celebrate Achievements:
Break Down Goals: Set achievable milestones and celebrate each accomplishment, no matter how small. Recognizing your progress provides a sense of achievement and keeps you motivated to reach the next milestone.

3. Stay Inspired:
Continuous Learning: Invest in your personal and professional development. Attend workshops, read books, or follow thought leaders in your industry. Learning new skills and gaining knowledge can reignite your passion.

Surround Yourself with Inspiration: Surround yourself with positive and motivated individuals. Engage with communities, attend networking events, or join online forums where you can share experiences and draw inspiration from others.

4. Practice Self-Care:

Rest and Renewal: Prioritize self-care activities, including adequate sleep, exercise, and relaxation. Taking care of your physical and mental well-being is crucial for sustaining motivation and creativity.

Mindfulness and Gratitude: Practice mindfulness and gratitude exercises. Being present and appreciating the positive aspects of your journey can enhance your overall sense of fulfillment.

5. Reward Yourself:

Celebrate Successes: Acknowledge your achievements and reward yourself for reaching significant milestones. Treat yourself to something special as a token of your hard work and dedication.

Remember, staying motivated is a continuous process that requires self-reflection, positive reinforcement, and a proactive approach to overcoming challenges. By adapting to market changes with resilience and staying motivated through self-care and inspiration, you'll not only sustain your side hustle but also thrive and achieve long-term success. Stay passionate, stay resilient, and keep your eyes on the goals that drive you forward.

Chapter 9

Scaling Your Side Hustle

Expanding Your Services

Scaling your side hustle means expanding your business operations to handle increased demand, reach a broader audience, and generate higher revenue. Here are strategies to effectively scale your side hustle:

1. Optimize Processes and Automation:

Efficiency is Key: Streamline your business processes to maximize efficiency. Identify bottlenecks and implement solutions to ensure smooth operations.

Automation Tools: Utilize automation tools for tasks like email marketing, customer communication, and social media posting. Automation saves time and allows you to focus on strategic aspects of your business.

2. Build a Strong Team:

Delegate Responsibly: As your side hustle grows, consider hiring employees or outsourcing tasks to skilled professionals. Delegate responsibilities to individuals who excel in specific areas, allowing you to concentrate on business development.

Cultivate Company Culture: Foster a positive work environment and instill a strong sense of purpose in your team. A motivated and engaged workforce contributes significantly to your side hustle's success.

3. Expand Your Online Presence:

E-commerce Platforms: If applicable, expand your online presence by selling your products on popular e-commerce platforms. Utilize platforms like Amazon, Etsy, or eBay to reach a broader customer base.

Social Media and Digital Marketing: Increase your social media presence and invest in digital marketing campaigns. Engage with your audience through social platforms and leverage targeted ads to expand your reach.

4. Collaboration and Partnerships:

Collaborate with Influencers: Partner with influencers or bloggers in your niche. Collaborations can significantly enhance your brand visibility and attract new customers.

Business Partnerships: Explore partnerships with complementary businesses. Joint ventures and collaborations can lead to mutual benefits, expanding your customer base and increasing revenue.

5. Monitor Financial Health:

Cash Flow Management: With increased business, keep a close eye on cash flow. Ensure you have adequate working capital to support the expanded operations and cover any unexpected expenses.

Profit Reinvestment: Reinvest a portion of your profits into further business growth. Allocate funds to marketing, research, and development, or launching new products/services.

Expanding Your Services: Offering More to Your Customers

Expanding your services allows you to cater to a wider range of customer needs and preferences. Here's how you can diversify and offer more to your customers:

1. Customer Surveys and Feedback:

Understand Customer Needs: Conduct surveys and gather feedback to understand what additional services or products your customers are interested in. Use this information to tailor your offerings.

2. Introduce New Products or Services:

Product Development: Innovate and create new products or services based on market demand and customer feedback. Launching new offerings can attract existing customers and draw in new ones.

Service Bundles: Package your existing services into bundles or packages. Bundling services offers value to customers and encourages them to engage with multiple services at once.

3. Upselling and Cross-selling:

Upselling: Encourage customers to upgrade to premium versions of your services. Highlight the added benefits and features they'll receive by opting for a higher-tier package.

Cross-selling: Identify complementary products or services that can be offered alongside your existing offerings. Cross-selling increases sales by introducing customers to related products they might find useful.

4. Focus on Customer Experience:

Exceptional Service: Provide exceptional customer service to create a positive experience. A satisfied customer is more likely to explore additional services and recommend your business to others.

Personalization: Personalize your offerings based on individual customer preferences. Tailored services enhance customer satisfaction and loyalty.

5. Promotions and Loyalty Programs:

Special Offers: Introduce limited-time promotions or discounts on new services to attract initial interest. Promotions can create a sense of urgency, prompting customers to try out the new offerings.

Loyalty Programs: Implement loyalty programs that reward customers for repeat business. Loyalty points, exclusive discounts, or members-only perks can encourage customers to explore your expanded services.

Expanding your side hustle requires careful planning, market research, and a customer-focused approach. By scaling efficiently, embracing new opportunities, and diversifying your offerings, you can sustain growth and provide enhanced value to your customers. Stay attentive to market trends, customer preferences, and feedback to guide your expansion efforts. With strategic decision-making and a commitment to customer satisfaction, your side hustle can thrive and evolve into a successful and sustainable business.

Growing Your Customer Base

Expanding your customer base is essential for the growth and sustainability of your side hustle. Here's how you can attract new customers and retain existing ones:

1. Define Your Target Audience:

Segmentation: Identify specific segments within your target market. Understand their needs, preferences, and pain points to tailor your marketing strategies effectively.

Market Research: Conduct market research to gain insights into your target audience. Analyze demographics, behavior, and buying patterns to refine your marketing approach.

2. Online Presence and Digital Marketing:

Professional Website: Ensure your website is user-friendly, visually appealing, and provides comprehensive information about your products or services.

SEO and Content Marketing: Optimize your website for search engines (SEO) and create valuable content related to your niche. Quality content establishes your expertise and attracts organic traffic.

Social Media Marketing: Leverage social media platforms to engage with potential customers. Consistent and engaging social media content can increase brand visibility and attract followers.

3. Customer Referral Program:

Incentivize Referrals: Encourage satisfied customers to refer your business to others by offering incentives such as discounts, exclusive offers, or loyalty points for successful referrals.

Word of Mouth: Provide exceptional products or services to ensure positive word-of-mouth marketing. Happy customers are more likely to recommend your business to their networks.

4. Networking and Partnerships:

Networking Events: Attend industry events, conferences, and trade shows to network with potential customers and other entrepreneurs. Personal connections can lead to valuable business opportunities.

Partnerships: Collaborate with other businesses or influencers in your niche. Partnerships can introduce your brand to a broader audience and create mutually beneficial relationships.

5. Excellent Customer Service:

Responsive Support: Provide prompt and helpful customer support. Address inquiries, concerns, and issues promptly. Excellent customer service builds trust and customer loyalty.

Feedback Utilization: Use customer feedback to improve your products, services, and overall customer experience. Listening to your customers enhances your offerings based on their needs.

Hiring Help and Outsourcing

As your side hustle grows, hiring help and outsourcing tasks become crucial for managing the increased workload and ensuring business efficiency:

1. Identify Areas for Help:

Assess Your Strengths: Determine tasks where you excel and focus on those. Identify tasks that can be delegated to others, such as administrative work, marketing, or customer service.

Critical Roles: Consider hiring experts for roles that are critical to your business's success, such as digital marketing specialists, web developers, or customer support professionals.

2. Hiring Employees:

Job Descriptions: Clearly define job roles, responsibilities, and qualifications when hiring employees. A well-written job description attracts suitable candidates.

Cultural Fit: Look for candidates who align with your business values and culture. A cohesive team fosters a positive work environment and enhances productivity.

3. Outsourcing Tasks:

Freelancers and Agencies: Outsource specific tasks to freelancers or agencies specializing in areas like graphic design, content writing, or social media management.

Benefits of Outsourcing: Outsourcing allows you to access specialized skills without the overhead costs of hiring full-time employees. It offers flexibility and scalability for your business.

4. Time Management and Oversight:

Effective Delegation: Delegate tasks based on team members' strengths and expertise. Communicate expectations and deadlines to ensure tasks are completed efficiently.

Regular Updates: Schedule regular check-ins or updates with your team members or outsourced partners. Open communication fosters collaboration and ensures everyone is aligned with your business goals.

5. Legal and Financial Considerations:

Contracts: Establish clear contracts with freelancers or agencies detailing the scope of work, timelines, and payment terms. Legal agreements provide clarity and protect both parties.

Financial Planning: Budget for hiring help and outsourcing. Consider the costs involved and ensure they align with your financial projections. Allocate funds strategically to optimize your resources.

Growing your customer base, hiring help, and outsourcing tasks are fundamental steps in scaling your side hustle effectively. By understanding your target audience, embracing digital marketing, providing exceptional customer service, and strategically delegating tasks, you can expand your business and focus on its core aspects. Remember, building a reliable team and nurturing customer relationships are key components of long-term success. Stay adaptable, maintain open communication, and invest in the growth of your side hustle to achieve sustainable expansion and profitability.

Chapter 10

Achieving Financial Freedom

Setting and Revising Financial Goals

Financial freedom is a goal that many aspire to achieve, and your side hustle can be a stepping stone toward that objective. Here's how you can work toward financial freedom through your side hustle:

1. Develop Multiple Income Streams: Diversify your income sources beyond your side hustle. Invest in stocks, real estate, or other passive income streams. Having multiple sources of income provides stability and financial security.

2. Manage Debt Wisely: Minimize and manage your debt effectively. Avoid high-interest debt and focus on paying off existing debts. Being debt-free or having manageable debts reduces financial stress and enhances your ability to invest.

3. Create an Emergency Fund: Establish an emergency fund that covers at least three to six months' worth of living expenses. An emergency fund acts as a financial safety net during unexpected situations, allowing you to maintain financial stability.

4. Save and Invest: Save a portion of your side hustle income and invest it wisely. Consider options like mutual funds, index funds, or retirement accounts. Regular saving and smart investing enable your money to grow over time.

5. Monitor Expenses: Keep a close eye on your expenses. Differentiate between essential and non-essential expenditures. Creating a budget and tracking your spending habits helps you identify areas where you can save more.

Setting and Revising Financial Goals: A Roadmap to Success

Setting clear financial goals provides direction and motivation for your financial journey. Here's how you can establish and revise your financial goals effectively:

1. Define Specific Goals:

Clarity: Clearly define your financial goals. Whether it's saving for a home, paying off debts, or retiring early, specificity provides a clear target to work toward.

Short-Term and Long-Term: Differentiate between short-term goals (accomplishable within a year) and long-term goals (achievable over several years). This helps you prioritize and plan accordingly.

2. Make Goals Achievable:

Realistic Targets: Ensure your goals are realistic and attainable. Consider your current financial situation, income, and expenses when setting the goals. Setting overly ambitious goals can lead to frustration.

3. Set Measurable Milestones:

Quantify Progress: Break down your goals into smaller, measurable milestones. Tracking progress provides a sense of accomplishment and motivates you to continue working toward your financial objectives.

Regular Evaluation: Regularly assess your progress against these milestones. Celebrate achievements and reevaluate if necessary. Adjust your goals based on changing circumstances or unexpected events.

4. Budget and Save:

Budgeting: Create a budget that allocates specific amounts to various expenses, savings, and investments. Budgeting helps you stay on track toward your financial goals.

Automate Savings: Automate your savings by setting up automatic transfers to a dedicated savings or investment account. Automating the process ensures consistency and discipline in saving.

5. Seek Professional Advice:

Financial Planner: If needed, consult a financial planner. A professional can help you set realistic goals, create a personalized financial plan, and provide expert advice on investments and wealth management.

6. Stay Adaptable:

Changing Goals: Life circumstances and priorities change. Be open to revising your financial goals as needed. Flexibility allows you to adapt to new opportunities and challenges.

7. Celebrate Achievements:

Acknowledge Progress: Celebrate your achievements, no matter how small. Recognizing your progress maintains motivation and encourages you to keep working toward your goals.

Setting and revising financial goals is an ongoing process that requires diligence and adaptability. By defining clear objectives, breaking them down into achievable milestones, and regularly evaluating your progress, you pave the way for financial freedom. Remember, financial freedom is not just about accumulating wealth; it's about having the freedom to make choices that align with your values and aspirations. Stay focused, stay disciplined, and take proactive steps toward securing your financial future through your side hustle journey.

Investing Your Side Hustle Earnings

Investing your side hustle earnings strategically can help you grow your wealth, create financial security, and achieve your long-term financial goals. Here are some key strategies to consider:

1. Diversify Your Investments:

Spread Risk: Diversification is the key to managing risk. Invest in a variety of assets, such as stocks, bonds, real estate, and mutual funds, to reduce the impact of a downturn in any one sector.

2. Consider Retirement Accounts:

Tax-Advantaged Savings: Contribute to retirement accounts like a 401(k) or an Individual Retirement Account (IRA). These accounts offer tax advantages, such as tax-deferred or tax-free growth, which can help you save more over time.

3. Invest in Passive Income Streams:

Real Estate Investments: Consider investing in real estate properties to generate rental income. Real estate can provide a reliable source of passive income.

Dividend Stocks: Invest in stocks of companies that pay regular dividends. Dividend income can be a consistent source of cash flow.

4. Regularly Reinvest Earnings:

Compound Earnings: Reinvest the earnings from your investments to benefit from the power of compounding. Over time, compounding can significantly boost your returns.

5. Monitor and Adjust:

Regular Evaluation: Keep an eye on your investments and assess their performance. If necessary, make adjustments to your portfolio to align with your financial goals and risk tolerance.

6. Seek Professional Advice:

Financial Advisor: Consider working with a financial advisor or planner who can provide guidance on investment strategies and help you make informed decisions.

Investing your side hustle earnings wisely can help you build wealth, generate passive income, and work toward achieving financial freedom.

Preparing for Full-Time Entrepreneurship

Transitioning from a side hustle to full-time entrepreneurship is a significant decision. Here's how you can prepare for this exciting journey:

1. Create a Detailed Business Plan:

Vision and Goals: Outline your business's long-term vision and specific goals. Define your niche, target market, and unique value proposition.

Financial Projections: Develop a detailed financial plan that includes income projections, expenses, and funding requirements.

2. Build a Financial Safety Net:

Emergency Fund: Ensure you have an adequate emergency fund to cover living expenses for at least three to six months. Having a financial cushion can reduce the stress associated with the transition.

3. Analyze Healthcare and Benefits:

Health Insurance: Research health insurance options for entrepreneurs. Understanding your healthcare coverage is crucial as you transition away from an employer's benefits.

4. Assess Legal and Tax Considerations:

Legal Structure: Determine the legal structure for your business, such as sole proprietorship, LLC, or corporation. Consult with legal and tax professionals to ensure compliance.

Tax Planning: Understand the tax implications of your business structure. Consider setting up an accounting system and tax plan to manage finances efficiently.

5. Network and Seek Mentors:

Networking: Build a strong professional network within your industry. Attend relevant events and connect with peers, potential collaborators, and mentors.

Mentorship: Seek mentorship from experienced entrepreneurs who can provide guidance, share insights, and help you navigate the challenges of full-time entrepreneurship.

6. Test the Waters:

Transition Period: Consider gradually reducing your hours at your current job to allow for a smoother transition. This can provide time to test the feasibility of your business as a full-time endeavor.

7. Continuous Learning:

Skills Development: Invest in skill development and business knowledge. Stay updated on industry trends and best practices to remain competitive in your field.

8. *Marketing and Branding:*

Establish Your Brand: Build a strong online presence and brand identity. Effective marketing is essential to attract customers and clients.

9. *Monitor Finances:*

Regular Budgeting: Continue budgeting your personal and business finances closely. Ensure you have a clear understanding of your financial health as a full-time entrepreneur.

Preparing for full-time entrepreneurship is an exciting yet challenging journey. By meticulously planning, building a financial safety net, seeking professional advice, and continuously learning and improving, you can increase your chances of success and navigate the transition effectively. This chapter serves as a roadmap for making a smooth and confident transition to full-time entrepreneurship with your side hustle.

Conclusion

Congratulations on reaching the end of this transformative guide, "How to Start a Side Hustle in 30 Days or Less: Learn How to Make Money Online, Become Your Boss, and Achieve Financial Freedom Through Freelancing, Dropshipping, and E-Commerce." We've embarked on an exhilarating journey together, exploring the intricacies of turning your passion and skills into a thriving side hustle and, ultimately, a pathway to financial freedom.

In the pages of this book, you've learned how to define your niche, conduct market research, and choose the right side hustle model tailored to your strengths and aspirations. You've delved into the realms of freelancing, dropshipping, and e-commerce, mastering the art of managing client relationships, finding profitable products, setting up online stores, and optimizing user experiences. We've discussed the importance of adapting to market changes, staying motivated, and overcoming challenges while balancing your side hustle with your full-time job.

You've discovered the significance of growing your customer base, hiring help, and outsourcing tasks to scale your side hustle efficiently. We've explored the essential concepts of financial freedom, setting and revising financial goals, investing wisely, and preparing for the exhilarating transition to full-time entrepreneurship. Armed with this knowledge and insight, you now possess the tools needed to take control of your financial destiny.

Remember, the journey to financial freedom is not a sprint; it's a marathon, and your side hustle is the vehicle that will propel you forward. It's about resilience, adaptability, and a steadfast commitment to your goals. As you venture into the world of entrepreneurship, keep in mind the lessons learned and the strategies outlined in this book. Embrace challenges as opportunities for growth, celebrate every milestone, and continuously seek knowledge and mentorship.

Your side hustle is not just a source of income; it's your ticket to independence, creativity, and fulfillment. With dedication, perseverance, and the insights gained from these pages, you have the power to shape your destiny, achieve financial freedom, and live the life you've always dreamed of.

Thank you for being a part of this journey. Now, go out there and make your dreams a reality. Your side hustle adventure awaits, and the path to financial freedom is yours to carve. Here's to your success, your freedom, and a future filled with endless possibilities. Start hustling, and let the world witness your brilliance!